Back To My Roots

SHARING RECIPES FROM THE VILLAGES OF GREECE

Krystina Kalapothakos
Kouzounas Kitchen

Interior formatter: Deborah Bradseth of Tugboat Design
Editor: Athina Pantazatou

"Back to My Roots" is inspired by my grandparents' village in Mani, Greece. It was my wish to share recipes from the area, by recreating them with my own twist.

Growing up in a Greek family, I learned how to cook at a young age. I was fascinated by phyllo dough and by the process of making *spanakopita* (Greek spinach pie).

My father is a landscaper and he is extremely passionate with his garden. At age seven, I would watch him tend to and enjoy his amazing garden. We have been lavender farmers for well over 15 years in Northern California. I never appreciated lavender in my teenage years, but after hearing my parents rant and rave about its benefits, I began to recognize its worth. I watched my mother make various recipes with lavender, and I began experimenting myself with assorted gourmet lavender recipes. In 2007 I attended Le Cordon Bleu, and graduated in 2008. I discovered a new found enthusiasm for lavender crème brûlée. The devotion to my pastry chef days inspired me to open up my own catering business; "Kouzounas Kitchen."

"Back to My Roots" is about going back to the days of robust village life and exploring the traditional Greek recipes of my grandparents. Greece

Mani, Greece
Featured Far Left- Yiayia, Father, Me, and Papou

offers a wide variety of healthy, delicious recipes that you can't often find these days. The Mediterranean diet has grown very popular in the past few years, and I am now here to share with you some of my family recipes that I find you will love.

DEDICATION

Kouzounas Kitchen is dedicated to my yiayia, Stavroula Kouzouna Kalapothakou. My parents tell me I resemble my yiayia not only in her looks, but in her love of cooking as well. I started blogging back in April of 2012, and had had the opportunity to interact with some fabulous food bloggers from all over the globe! Today I share recipes from around the world in my food group called Foodify, as well as on my food blog called Kouzounas Kitchen. I hope you enjoy this book as much as I did creating it.

~I dedicate this book to my family, especially to my yiayia whom I love and miss dearly. ~

I would like to thank the following people for their time, wonderful support, and dedication to this book, but most importantly for their huge hearts and determination in helping me make Kouzounas Kitchen Cookbook a success.

Angela Santarelli, Athina Pantazatou of "Kicking Back the Pebbles", Chef Danny, Chef Stephanie, Chef Tony, Christine Tsalavoutas of "Christine It", Despina Kreatsoulas of "Politismos", Diana Juarez of "LD Juarez", Dianne Hinaris of "The Olive Table", Effie Speyer of "Cheffie's Kitchen", Ekaterina Botziou of "The Greek Wives Club", Elaine Boddy of "Foodbod", Eleni Anagnostopoulou of "My Easy Gourmet", Friends Of The Earth Lavender, Gina Zarcadoolas of "Foodie WineLover", Giorgos Milonas of "Jnk Artworks", Jeannette R., Katina Vaselopoulos of "Journeys with Katina", Kelly K., Larry L., Leilani D., Nestor Zaharopoulos of Nestor Z Photography, Panayiotis Galanis of "CyTasty", Paula F., Stephanie B., Stephen Liddell, Terrald Bright, the brands Nescafe and Athens Phyllo, the Kalapothakos family, my nephew Kase, the Kouzounas family, the Manansala family, the Zaharopoulos family, Foodify, and Kouzounas Kitchen fans. Of course a huge thank you goes out to those who featured their recipes in this book.

The places listed below are also very dear to me and an integral part of my inspiration:

Mani	Skiathos
Athens	Lefkada
Parasyros	Sacramento
Kotronas	

TABLE OF CONTENTS

History of Olive Oil
Η Ιστορία του Ελαιόλαδου

We have to pay homage to the ancient Greeks for many wonderful reasons, but one is for food and wine alone!

The ancient Greeks consumed bread and wine with many of their courses. Breakfast consisted of bread dipped in wine, while lunch consisted of bread, wine, cheese, figs, and olives. (You see why we love our bread, right?!) For dinner, they consumed many vegetables, fish, fruit, and possibly cakes made of honey. Sugar did not exist at the time, so the Greeks would use honey as their main sweetener. They also consumed many fish, as their main source of protein. Beef was rarely consumed as it was very expensive and only on certain occasions did the ancient Greeks eat beef and pork!

In these ancient times, Greek people had the bare minimum of cooking utensils. Most of the utensils were made out of unglazed or partly glazed clay. Spoons and knives were common, but forks were not even heard of. Greeks would use bread to scoop up many of their foods, or to dip in sauces. After they ate, they would clean their hands with bread.

Wine was the main drink, along with water of course. Wine was very popular and Greece is one of the oldest wine producing countries in the world (going as far back as 6500 years). Not only did Greeks produce wine, they also expanded their vineyards throughout Europe in France, Italy, Austria and many other countries. Most of the wine that was being produced was sweet and aromatic and came in variety of colors (black, red, white).

Wine was also being used to kill bacteria from stagnant drinking water that usually came from nearby streams and rivers. Theophrastus [Theofrass-tus] was a scholar of the Aristotelian school, fascinated with wine and winemaking! He was one of the first to make observations on how to grow the vines and on what kind of soil should be used in order to produce high quality wine, leaving a detailed record of influences and innovations in viticulture. "Food without wine is a corpse; wine without food is a ghost; united and well matched they are as body and soul, living partners." – Andre Simon (1877-1970)

Back in 3500 B.C., in the early Minoan stages in Crete – Greece, olive trees were cultivated for the first time worldwide! By 2000 B.C. olive trees were playing an important role on the island's economy. The first export of the olive tree soon brought it to Northern Africa and to the Asia Minor.

The olive tree has ever since been a symbol of peace and wisdom in Greece, and it is the sacred tree of the city of Athens. Winners in the Ancient Olympic Games were presented with an olive oil wreath made from branches cut from a wild olive tree.

Source: Pomeroy, Sarah B. Ancient Greece. New York: Oxford University Press, 1999

"The olive oil tree is surely the richest gift of heaven."
-Thomas Jefferson

Top Health Benefits of Olive Oil

• Lowers Cholesterol
Olive oil increases HDL (High-Density Lipoprotein) cholesterol in the body. This plays a protective role and helps prevent blood clotting -the key reason behind heart attacks and strokes.

• Reduces High Blood Sugar
Researchers believe that the oleic acid in olive oil is easily absorbed in the body, thereby lowering blood pressure.

• Fights Diabetes
Olive oil is believed to improve the blood sugar and to control and enhance insulin sensitivity. Additionally, the monounsaturated fats in olive oil help keep triglyceride levels in check.

This "miracle" ingredient can be used in many ways to reap lots of its benefits as it:

• Improves brain function
• Fights inflammation
• Aids weight loss
• Rejuvenates the skin
• Improves hair health

"If my cuisine were to be defined by just one taste, it would be that of subtle, aromatic, extra-virgin olive oil."
- Alain Ducasse

Measurement Standards

COMMON COOKING EQUIVALENCES

1 PINCH	⟷	1/8 TSP
1 DRY OUNCE	⟷	1/16 POUND
1 POUND	⟷	16 OUNCES
1 TEASPOON	⟷	1/3 TABLESPOON
1 TABLESPOON	⟷	3 TEASPOONS
1 FLUID OUNCE	⟷	1/8 CUP
1/4 CUP	⟷	4 TABLESPOONS
1 CUP	⟷	8 FLUID OUNCES
1 PINT	⟷	2 CUPS
1 QUART	⟷	2 PINTS
1 GALLON	⟷	4 QUARTS

As much as I loved to travel, it had always been hard for me to cook outside my kitchen since I was only familiar to the standard US measurements. I especially appreciated travelling to Greece because I had to learn the metric system. I slowly began to learn how to convert from US measurements to Metric. I hope this excerpt of oven-degree conversions helps those of you who might be in my shoes one day, and will need to convert temperatures.

Oven Temperatures – Fahrenheit to Celsius
U.S. to Metric Conversions

225 °F	110 °C	375 °F	190 °C
250 °F	130 °C	400 °F	200 °C
275 °F	140 °C	425 °F	220 °C
300 °F	150 °C	450 °F	230 °C
325 °F	170 °C	475 °F	240 °C
350 °F	180 °C	500 °F	250 °C

Kouzounas Kitchen Pantry Ingredients

Most of the ingredients I use, in each of my recipes, are readily available at super markets and grocery stores. However, some ingredients or cooking terms might be unclear to "beginners," so I created the list below to assist you further.

Greek Extra Virgin Olive Oil: The best olive oil to cook with. Cold pressed without any chemicals added to the process.

Honey: Clove or thyme honey

Phyllo Dough: Very thin dough, used to make savory and sweet pies.

Feta Cheese: This is the most common cheese used in Greek cuisine. It is made with sheep's milk, or with a mixture of sheep (≥70%) and (≥30%) goat milk. Feta means "slice". My favorite cheese by far!

Ouzo: My favorite Greek liquor. Ouzo has a very distinct anise aroma. Ouzo is traditionally mixed with water, to create a cloud like effect and it is usually served on ice.

Trahanas: Course ground Greek pasta made from semolina grain. You can find this product at any Greek market in your city.

Semolina: Wheat used in making pasta, cereal, puddings, and desserts. You can find semolina at local international markets.

Measurement Lingo
When following each recipe, please keep in mind of the teaspoon/tablespoon abbreviations below:
Teaspoon = tsp
Tablespoon = TB

Things experience has taught me (multiple times!):

Always make sure you read your recipe first to ensure that you have all the ingredients in the kitchen.

If you want to improvise on an ingredient, make sure you do your research first and see if you can use a replacement.

If you are unsure of a spice in your recipe, research the spice and understand what kind of flavors it gives off.

Use a microplane grater to shave vegetables and fruit into salads for added flavor (my favorites are ginger and orange).

When baking cakes avoid opening the oven door, as the cold air will interfere with the rising of the cake.

While making cookies, remove butter and cream cheese from the refrigerator to soften, prior to baking.

Marinate foods in the refrigerator, not at room temperature.

Wine should be stored in a cool place of a temperature between 45-65°F. Store wine away from light and vibration.

Pairing Wines

Pair bold red wines with red meats (Cabernet Sauvignon, Pinot Noir, Zinfandel and Syrah).

Pair lighter white wines with vegetables (Pinot Grigio, Sauvignon Blanc and Albarino).

When in doubt, sparkling wine goes with everything!

Pair dessert wines with chocolate or any sweet sauces (Port, Sherry and Tokaji).

THE OLIVE TABLE

"The Olive Table imports premium extra virgin olive oils from our family groves in Messenia, Greece and raw all natural honey from Peloponnese. Our oils are cold extracted from 100% Koroneiki olives and include a smooth, delicate intensity Private Reserve and a more robust Organic Early Harvest. Our honey varieties include unique 'forest' honey such as Fir and Pine, as well as Chestnut, Oak, Orange Blossom and Mediterranean Heather. We are a 'boutique' service-oriented company focused on the freshness, purity and quality of our authentic Greek products. Contact us at info@theolivetable.com for information on retail or wholesale purchases of our premium Greek extra virgin olive oils and raw all natural honey. Visit our website at theolivetable.com."

THE
Olive
TABLE

EXTRA VIRGIN OLIVE OIL
KYPARISSIA GREECE

SINGLE ESTATE - HANDPICKED

PRIVATE RESERVE

500 ML (16.9 FL OZ)

THE
Olive
TABLE

ORGANIC
EXTRA VIRGIN OLIVE OIL
CHRISTIANOUPOLIS GREECE

EARLY HARVEST - HANDPICKED

SINGLE ESTATE

500 ML (16.9 FL OZ)

My angel who is always watching over me from heaven is my yiayia Stavroula. I know I can endure rough times because she reminds me what strength and perseverance is. I can feel her presence as I am cooking in my kitchen. One scent I can continuously smell in the air is the warm milk yiayia used to boil while making coffee.

Many people take one glance at me and tell me that I am a spitting image of my sweet yiayia. Perhaps I was designed to walk in her footsteps, and carry on the love she had for cooking. I also feel I was meant to share her traditional Greek recipes with the world. Whatever it may be, I know she is always here with me in spirit. Every time I go to Greece, I visit our village in Parasyros, and I feel that she is there smiling.

Unfortunately, I lost my loving yiayia to cancer, as well as my papou (grandfather) and my two uncles. My father is the only person left who remains healthy and strong. It was and still is very difficult to lose our family members, as they were such a huge part of my life while growing up. We've also lost all of my grandparents' siblings, and I wish I could have met them! Cancer seems to take away all the beautiful people in this world including my family. Even through tragedy, I am grateful I can share the memories I have with them in this cookbook.

I remember my yiayia used to take my hand to the periptero (kiosk) in Athens and buy me gum or candy. She always watched over me, and I am just so grateful to her for everything she did.

Kouzounas Kitchen comes from my yiayia's maiden last name. Please don't confuse with "kouzina" which means kitchen in Greek.

POLITISMOS

Co Founders: Despina M. Kreatsoulas &
Thanos Chinis

This cookbook shares not only recipes, but a family history. We like to think that each family history is like one of the many beautiful threads woven into the fascinating and intricate tapestry of Greek history! To learn more about the Greece and its people - from antiquity to modernity - we invite you to visit www.PolitismosMuseum.org

Follow us on
Facebook: PolitismosMuseum
Twitter: @PolitismosGRUSA
Instagram: PolitismosMuseum

Let's Learn Some Greek
Ας μάθουμε Ελληνικά!

Words

Family: Οικογένεια
[e-ko-ge-néa]

Love: Αγάπη [a-ga-pé]

Church: Εκκλησία [e-klé-sia]

Ouzo: Ούζο

Frappe: Φραπέ

Freddo: Φρέντο

Greek Salad: Χωριάτικη Σαλάτα
[ho-ria-té-ké sa-la-ta]

Dance: Χορός [ho-ros]

Party: Γιορτή [yior-tè]

Beach: Παραλία [pa-ra-léa]

Friends: Φίλοι [fee-lee]

Coffee: Καφές [ka-fes]

Music: Μουσική [mou-sé-ké]

Gyro: Γύρος

Olives: Ελιές [e-lies]

Phrases

Γεια σου! [yah-soo] Hello!

Τι κάνεις – Τι κάνετε;
[tee kah-nés? – tee kah-neh-teh?]
How are you?
(Singular and plural)

Καλά, ευχαριστώ!
[kah-lah ef-hah-rees-toh]
I am fine, thank you!

Παρακαλώ [pah-rah-kah-loh]
You're welcome or please
(double meaning)

Ευχαριστώ! [eff-hah-rees-toh]
Thank you!

Ναι [neh]
Yes

Όχι [oh-hee]
No

Καλημέρα [kah-lee-meh-rah]
Good Morning!

Καλησπέρα
 [kah-lee-speh-rah]
Good evening!

Phrases (continued)

Καληνύχτα
[kah-lee-neeh-tah]
Good night!

Πως σε/σας λένε;
[pohs seh/sas leh-neh?]
What is your name? (Singular
and plural)

Ένα φλιτζάνι [ena flee-t-zané]
One/A cup

Θέλω να μαγειρέψω.
[thélo na ma-gé-rè-pso]
 I want to cook

Despite being born and raised in the USA, as a little child, I was very exposed to the Greek language. Was it easy for me? NO WAY! Do I love the language? YES! My father had my younger sister and me, enrolled in private Greek lessons when we were about 9 and 11 years old. To be honest with you the only reason I loved these Greek lessons was because I enjoyed the Greek sweets we got from Mrs. R, our Greek teacher. (Shhh, don't tell her please!).

Later on, in my teenage years, I had a hard time communicating with my family in Greece when we went on family trips to Mani. I was often overwhelmed by a sense of embarrassment when I couldn't really communicate with my cousins and all I could say were the basics. But I think that what really did it for me was when I went back to Greece in 2009: I was staying at a friend's house in Piraeus and my cousin Panayiotis, on my *yiayia's* side of the family, came to meet me. He didn't pick me up from the house but we met at a central place instead. We had planned to go out for coffee and I was so excited to meet him that I didn't even think to write down the address I was staying at! So, have you ever been in the awkward situation of having to "speak" with your hands and not being able to understand another person (or they, you) while confronted with a different language?!! This happened to my cousin and me, but for some reason it all worked out while we were at the coffee shop. It was hard but it was fun and, after all, I was in Greece and I wanted to learn more of the language. The real problem surfaced when it was time to go home! I couldn't remember the Greek name of the address to my friend's house. My poor cousin tried really hard to understand my terrible directions in English, but we couldn't find the place no matter what. At that point I really needed a translator! We found the house after driving around in circles for about 45 minutes... It was then when I decided that it was truly important for me to learn Greek.

I decided to set that goal and learn the language in Greece. I enrolled to attend the University of Athens on the same year (2009). I remember having a really hard time when I took the placement test, and I was placed in Beta Ena (B1) which was intermediate Greek. I will never forget the first day of classes, when my teacher said "Okay students, we are only going to speak Greek in this class." My mouth literally dropped on the floor, and I felt overwhelmed with embarrassment once again. Just to give you an idea, I was the only Greek-American in the class. All the other students were non-Greeks, living and working in Greece and needing to know how to speak the language. This, of course, was not just a conversational language class but we were also taught how to write. Okay, let me just say here, writing in Greek is very difficult! Did you all know the "alphabet" word itself comes from the first two letters of the Greek alphabet?

Back in 2012 I was visiting my boyfriend who lived in Athens, Greece at the time. We were walking around the city and for some reason this sign got my attention, so I had to snap a photo.

Speaking of Greek beer... Did you know that in Ancient Greece, beer wasn't produced domestically, but it was still enjoyed by the Greeks? The ancient Greeks were huge fans of blonde beer which was imported from various countries. They were however more keen on their wine than on their beer, as the latter was partially considered some sort of a lower-class beverage since it was fairly easy to make and despite the fact that it was a bit expensive!

Nowadays, the most popular beer brands in Greece include:

Mythos – a blonde lager produced by Mythos Brewery.

Volkan – this is an interesting mix of Santorini honey and Naxos citron.

Fix – the vintage of Greek beers.

Alfa – a blonde lager which is on the lighter side. Produced by the Athenian Brewery.

Bios 5 – the world's first beer produced with 5 grains! Brewed by the Athenian Brewery.

Neda – this beer is named after the Greek goddess Neda, goddess of water. Produced in Messinia.

Marathon – an exclusive lager that is really popular.

Yiayia Stavroula not only had a love for cooking, but she had a smile on her face every time she was in her kitchen making something delicious. When you truly love something and have a real passion for it, whatever it may be, this passion shines through.

My yiayia loved making many different kinds of authentic Greek recipes, and she learned how to make the majority of these when she was a young girl. Growing up in the village, surrounded by many siblings, she learned the art of cooking through survival instincts.

My father would tell me stories about my grandmother's joy of putting even something as simple as a homemade loaf of bread on the dinner table.

Yiayia Stavroula was born in the 1920's and she survived World War II by hiding out in the village of Kotrona. She gave birth to my dad in 1944. Although my yiayia never had a lot of food for her own family, she always made sure that friends and neighbors who walked through her door had food on *their* plate. She had a magical way of making a beautiful, tasting meal with only a few simple ingredients.

Appetizers
Μεζέδες

Σπανακόπιτα
Greek Spinach Pie [Spanakopita]

YIELD: 25 PIECES

1/2	cup olive oil
2	garlic cloves, minced
1	cup fresh dill, chopped
6	scallions, finely chopped
3	pounds fresh spinach
	Salt and pepper
2	tsp of cumin
1/2	cup basil, minced
1/2	cup anise, minced
1/2	cup parsley, minced
1/2	cup mint, minced
6	ounces feta cheese
2	large eggs, beaten
1/2	cup condensed unsweetened milk
2	sticks unsalted butter, melted
1	package phyllo

1. Heat olive oil in a large skillet over medium-high heat. Add your garlic, fresh herbs, scallions, and leeks. Cook, stirring, until scallions and leeks are soft and translucent, about 5 minutes.

2. Cook your spinach on medium heat and let it simmer for about 10 minutes. Remove from heat and add it to your herb mixture. Add feta to your spinach and herb mixture. Make sure it has cooled down before you add in your beaten eggs. Mix in the condensed milk and whisk. Now add in your salt, pepper and cumin. Set aside in the fridge.

3. Brush a large baking dish with butter. Trim the phyllo to the size of the pan. Work quickly and keep the remaining phyllo covered with a plastic wrap, topped with a warm towel to keep it moist: place one sheet of phyllo on the baking dish you've prepared and brush it with butter; top with another sheet. Repeat process until you have 10 sheets of phyllo in the baking dish.

4. When you have used half the phyllo sheets, pour the spinach mixture in the dish. Add the remaining layers of phyllo over the top.

5. Make sure you brush the top layer with butter or olive oil. Score the top phyllo layers in triangles.

6. Preheat the oven to 375°F. Cook for about 45 minutes, until the phyllo is golden brown. Remove from the oven and let it cool.

Ταπενάντ με Ελιές Καλαμών
Kalamata Olive Tapenade

YIELD: 4 SERVINGS

5   cups Kalamata olives
1   TB capers
1   lemon (juice)
2   cloves garlic
2   tsp thyme
2   tsp oregano
1/2   cup olive oil
     Pinch red pepper
     Fresh ground pepper
5   cups lady fingers or cherry tomatoes
     Fresh mint to sprinkle with

1. In a food processor combine all ingredients except tomatoes.

2. Pulse until ingredients are well combined.

3. Cut tomatoes in half and scoop out tomato seeds.

4. Add to the mix and chill for about 2 hours so flavors can combine.

Τυροπιτάκια Σφολιάτας
Mini Phyllo Cheese Bites

YIELD: 12 BITES

1	12-cup muffin pan, greased
12	sheets phyllo dough
2	eggs, beaten
2	TB olive oil
1/4	cup scallions, diced
1	cup cream cheese
3	TB Parmesan cheese
1/2	cup feta cheese
	Pinch of Herbs De Provence
	Pinch of dried dill
	Sea salt & pepper

1. In a large bowl add eggs, olive oil, scallions, cream cheese, Parmesan, feta, and spices. Whisk together and make sure ingredients are combined.

2. Turn oven temperature on 400°F.

3. Open up 12 phyllo sheets, and lay over a damp towel to prevent from drying.

4. Cut large circles out of each phyllo dough sheet. You should be able to get 2 circles out of each sheet.

5. Place one circle into the muffin pan and then lightly brush olive oil over the phyllo.

6. Repeat with another circle of phyllo over the top.

7. Once you have filled the muffin pan with phyllo (2 layers per cup), place a heaping tablespoon of filling into each phyllo cup. You can then fold the excess phyllo over the top of the cheese filling.

8. Bake in oven for approximately 30 minutes or until golden brown on top.

Κρέπες με Σπανάκι & Φέτα
Spinach & Feta Crepes

YIELD: 4 SERVINGS

1	cup all-purpose flour
1	TB granulated sugar
1/4	tsp Himalayan salt
1/2	cup coconut milk
2/3	cup water
1/4	cup butter, melted
1	TB vanilla extract

(vanilla is added, only if the mixture is intended for sweet crepes, not for savory, so you won't need it for this recipe)

1	cup spinach, sautéed
1/4	cup feta cheese, crumbled
	Pinch of dried oregano/basil

1. In a large bowl, mix the flour, sugar, and salt. Next mix the liquids together (coconut milk, water, butter).

2. Add the wet ingredients to the dry ingredients and whisk until all combined.

3. Prepare your skillet and warm it up over medium heat. Melt butter in pan.

4. Place about two tablespoons of the batter onto the pan, making sure you spread the batter around in a thin layer.

5. Let the crepe cook until the edges begin to lift, then flip to cook the other side.

6. Repeat with remaining batter and place crepes on a plate.

7. You can reheat crepes in the oven, at about 200°F for a few minutes.

8. To fill crepes, place a good amount of sautéed spinach in the center and add feta cheese. I like to sprinkle dried herbs over the mixture, and fold the crepe.

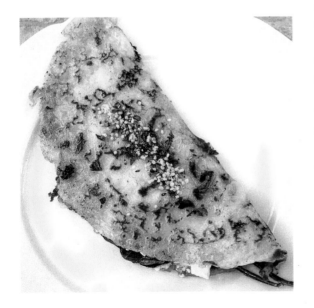

Γλυκά Ρολά
Sweet Rolls

YIELD: 12 ROLLS

1/2	cup water
1/2	cup milk
1	egg
1/3	cup butter, softened
1/3	cup honey
1	tsp Himalayan salt
3 3/4	cups all-purpose flour
1	package active dry yeast
1/4	cup butter, softened

1. Place water & milk in a microwave for about a minute and a half. Pour liquid into a mixer, add the sugar and stir to dissolve.

2. Add the yeast into the sugar mixture and make sure you whisk continuously until it foams and bubbles (about ten minutes).

3. Using your paddle attachment, mix on low speed and then add the salt, butter, and egg. Once you have mixed all your ingredients, add your flour in slowly. Change to the dough hook and knead for about 7 minutes, or until the dough is smooth.

4. Remove dough from the bowl and lightly flour a working surface. Cut the ball of dough into quarters and then roll each piece of dough into a ball. Place in a baking pan. Cover your baking pan with plastic wrap and let the dough sit for about one hour in a warm place. You want the rolls to rise. Then turn your oven on 400°F and brush each ball of dough with butter. Bake the rolls for about 10-15 minutes or until golden brown.

Στραπατσάδα
Tomato & Egg Scramble [Strapatsada]

YIELD: 2 SERVINGS

4	eggs
2	large tomatoes
1	tsp honey
2	TB olive oil
1	garlic clove, minced
2	tsp dried oregano
2	tsp dried basil
1/2	cup feta
	Parsley, chopped
	Salt & pepper to taste

1. Cut off the base of the tomato, and grate the tomato using a hand grater (you can also finely chop the tomato, if you don't have a grater).

2. In a large frying pan, add olive oil and garlic over medium heat. Sauté for one minute. Add tomatoes, garlic, and honey. Cook down the liquid, for about 8 minutes.

3. Whisk the eggs in a medium bowl, and add spices and seasonings. Stir the eggs into the tomato mixture and remove when eggs are cooked.

4. Sprinkle with feta cheese and parsley on top before you serve.

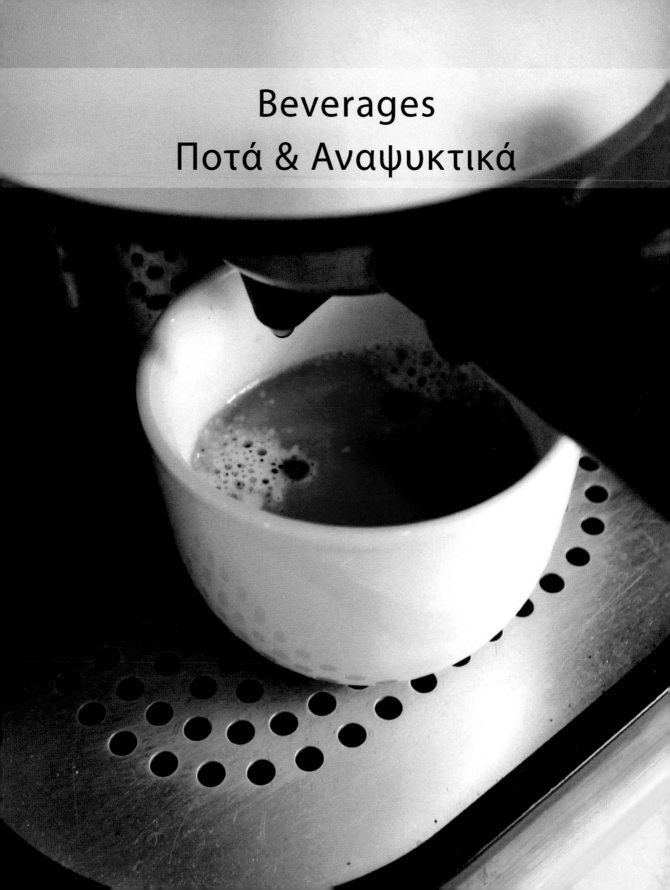

Beverages
Ποτά & Αναψυκτικά

Καφές Φραπέ
Frappe Coffee

SERVES: 1

3 tsp Nescafe (instant) coffee
2 tsp sugar (depending on how sweet you like it.)
Water
Ice cubes

1. In a shaker, combine instant coffee, sugar, 3 tablespoons of water, and shake for about 30 seconds.

2. Pour into a tall glass and add ice cold water, and ice cubes.

For a fun "Greek Frappe" add 2 tablespoons of Baileys and follow the directions above. That's my favorite summer Greek iced coffee!

Καπουτσίνο Φρέντο
Cappuccino Freddo

SERVES: 1   WRITTEN BY: KICKING BACK THE PEBBLES (ATHINA PANTAZATOU)

Espresso ground coffee
Evaporated milk
Sugar (optional)
Ice cubes
Cinnamon (optional)

Tools: an espresso machine & a milk frother

1. Take the two-shot filter basket. Fill it up with your favorite variety of espresso ground coffee and press it firmly. *(Or use two pods if that's what your machine takes).

2. Place the filter basket in the portafilter, hook it in place and make your espresso as usual.

3. Add any sugar you take in your coffee at this point and stir it well.

4. Fill a tall glass with ice. Pour your espresso in the glass. Throw two more ice cubes in your milk frother cup and pour in 3/4 cups of milk. You can use full-fat (whole), semi-skimmed or evaporated milk.

5. Froth the milk and add it to the coffee. Sprinkle with some cinnamon and enjoy.

Athina, a great friend and blogger at Kicking Back the Pebbles, resides in Greece. She has really inspired me to keep going with Kouzounas Kitchen, and I have to thank her for that. Her blog is bilingual (she writes in English & in Greek) and she shares wonderful Greek recipes, small DIYs and home-organization tips and tricks. Check out www.kickingbackthepebbles.com for more amazing recipes!

Ellènikos Kafes
Greek Coffee

SERVES: 1-2

How Sweet Do You Like Your Greek Coffee?
Sketos: Unsweetened
Metrios: Slightly sweet. Add 1 teaspoon of sugar (most popular).
Glykos: Very sweet coffee. Add 2 teaspoons of sugar.

Greek coffee
(Bravo or Loumidis are two very common brands)

Sugar (optional)

A *briki* (a small pot designed specifically to make Greek coffee. The body and handle are traditionally made of brass or copper, though nowadays they are also made from stainless steel)

Water

Demitasse cups

1. Depending on how many cups you are serving, measure out water accordingly and fill in a *briki* (I don't recommend doing more than 2 per turn).

2. Add 1 heaping teaspoon of Greek coffee per cup in the *briki*. (Add sugar if you like.)

3. Place *briki* on stove over medium-high heat. Stir gently making sure the sugar has dissolved.

4. Let the coffee come to a boil and create a thick foam on the surface. Serve immediately in demitasse cups.

"Μαρτίνι" με Ούζο & Λεμονάδα
Ouzo Lemonade Martini

SERVES: 2

2 cups ginger lemonade
  (follow Summer Lemonade recipe)
3 TB ouzo
4 ice cubes
1 martini shaker
1 lavender sprig

1. Place lemonade, ouzo, and ice cubes in a martini shaker or blender.

2. Shake until the mix foams.

3. Pour into a glass and serve with a fresh lavender sprig on top.

Καλοκαιρινή Λεμονάδα
Summer Lemonade

SERVES: 4

2	limes
2	lemons
8	cups cold water
3/4	cup sugar
3	TB fresh ginger
1	sprig fresh mint
4	ice cubes

1. In a blender, place limes, lemons, 4 cups water, and sugar on high speed.

2. Blend until limes and lemons are completely and thoroughly mixed.

3. Strain the mixture and place liquid back in blender. Add remaining water.

4. Serve over ice cubes and fresh mint. (If you want a slushy-like lemonade, add the ice cubes while blending the mix).

Please keep in mind that you are using whole lemons and limes, and if you use more than the recommended serving above, the lemonade might turn out too tart

"The fruits of life fall into the hands of those
who climb the tree and pick them."
– Earl Tupper (1907-1983)

Desserts
Επιδόρπια & Γλυκά

Greek Walnut Cake, pg 45

Κουραμπιέδες
Greek Christmas Cookies [Kourambiedes]

YIELD: 50 COOKIES

2	cups butter
1	cup confectioner's sugar
2	egg yolks
1	tsp baking powder
1	tsp baking soda
1/4	ztsp salt
1	TB brandy
1 1/2	tsp vanilla powder
3 1/2	cups all-purpose flour
1 1/2	cups toasted almonds, chopped
	Extra confectioner's sugar

Kourambiedes are perfect winter cookies! To make a peppermint filling flavor, add peppermint candies to the center of the dough, and fold the dough over.

1. Cream the butter and sugar in the mixer bowl for 18 minutes. Mix in the baking powder, baking soda, and salt.

2. Add the egg yolks, brandy, vanilla, and slowly add in the flour and almonds.

3. Let the dough stand for 30 minutes at room temperature (cover and set aside).

4. Pick up 1 1/2 teaspoons of dough and form round balls. Place dough on a buttered pan.

5. Bake at 350°F for 15 minutes, or until golden brown.

6. After removing the cookies out of the oven, spray them with ouzo.

7. Cover the cookies with confectioner's sugar.

Λουκουμάδες
Greek Doughnuts [Loukoumades]

YIELD: 70 PIECES

4	cups all-purpose flour
2	TB active dry yeast
1/2	tsp kosher salt
1	tsp vanilla powder
2	cups lukewarm milk-water (mixed)
1	cup honey
	Vegetable oil for frying
	Cinnamon for dusting
1	cup chopped walnuts, to sprinkle on top

1. In a large mixing bowl, dissolve the yeast in 1 cup of warm milk-water mixture. Cover the bowl with a towel, and let sit for 10 minutes, until the yeast bubbles on the surface.

2. In a bowl mix the flour, salt, and vanilla together.

3. Add the flour to the yeast in three stages, and add the remaining cup of milk-water to the mixture until you form a sticky dough. Cover the bowl and let mixture rise until doubled.

4. When the dough has doubled in size, heat the oil in a fryer.

5. This is the tricky part of the recipe. Make sure you have a glass of water, and a spoon handy. Dip your spoon into the water, then scoop a spoonful of dough (a "ball") and drop it into the fryer, one at a time. Make sure you always dip your spoon into the water so you prevent the dough from sticking to the spoon.

6. I fry about 5-7 balls of loukoumades at a time, since my fryer isn't very big. Once each side puffs up, and turns golden brown they are ready.

7. Drain the oil from the loukoumades (use a skimmer ladle to fish them out of the fryer), and set on a lined baking sheet (I line my baking sheet with paper towels so the oil can be absorbed). Once you fry all of the dough, place doughnuts in a large platter.

8. It's time to bring in the sweetness! Drizzle honey over the top and add chopped walnuts. I also sprinkle with a pinch of cinnamon powder before I serve.

Loukoumades have been around for some time, typically served at many Greek bakeries. They are basically a fried Greek doughnut covered in honey, walnuts, and cinnamon. Try serving these with vanilla ice cream to make your taste buds jump!

Καρυδόπιτα
Greek Walnut Cake [Karidopita]

YIELD: 25 PIECES

8	eggs, separated	2	cups water
1	cup sugar	2	cups sugar
1	tsp vanilla	1/2	cup honey
12	wheat crackers	2	strips orange peel
2/3	lb. walnuts	2	strips lemon peel
4	tsp cinnamon	1	cinnamon stick
1/4	tsp ground cloves		
1	tsp baking powder		
1/4	tsp salt		
1	tsp orange zest		
1	tsp lemon zest		

1. Preheat the oven to 350°F and grease a 9 by 13 baking dish.

2. Use mixer to beat egg whites until stiff. Then place the egg yolks inside another mixer bowl, and beat with sugar until yellow and pale in color. Add vanilla.

3. Next grind the wheat crackers into a food processor. Add in the walnuts and pulse until they are crushed into small pieces. Place the crumb mixture into a medium size bowl and add in cinnamon, baking powder, salt, cloves, lemon & orange zest. Add in the egg yolk mixture and stir. Slowly fold in the egg whites in 3 different additions.

4. Pour the batter into a non-stick baking dish and smooth out with a spatula. Bake for about 35 minutes or until golden on top. When syrup is done, remove cake from oven and pour syrup over the cake. Let the syrup soak into the cake.

Syrup

1. Combine the water, sugar, honey, orange - lemon peels and cinnamon stick in a saucepan.

2. Bring the mixture to a boil and simmer for about 10 minutes. Let the syrup cool down then remove the cinnamon stick and peels.

3. Pour syrup over cake and let the cake cool before serving.

Υγιεινή Μους Λεμονιού
Healthy Greek Lemon Mousse

YIELD: 8 RAMEKINS

1	cup plain Greek yogurt
2	tsp lemon zest
3	TB lemon juice (fresh)
1	tsp vanilla extract
1/4	cup water
1	sachet Knox gelatin (unflavored)
2/3	cup egg whites
	Pinch of salt
3/4	cup sugar

8 ramekin bowls

1. In a medium-size bowl combine yogurt, zest, juice, and vanilla extract. Whisk ingredients together and set aside.

2. Place water inside a small bowl. Sprinkle in the gelatin powder and set aside.

3. Fill in half a medium-size saucepan with water. Boil the water over medium high heat.

4. Throw egg whites, salt, and sugar into a mixer bowl. Stir the mixture gently to combine.

5. Place the mixer bowl into the pan of boiling water, and whisk the mixture gently until the sugar is dissolved.

6. Remove the bowl from the pan and pour the gelatin water into the egg mixture. Whisk quickly to combine the ingredients together.

7. Place bowl securely into position in the stand mixer. Using the whisk attachment, whip the egg mixture on medium to high speed for about 7 minutes.

8. Add in the Greek yogurt and continue whipping until the mixture is combined.

9. Divide the mixture among 8 ramekins and chill for at least one hour.

10. Serve cold with some fresh lemon zest on top or fresh berries.

Τα Μελομακάρονα της Θείας Μαρίας
Honey Dipped Cinnamon Cookies (Thea Maria's Melomakarona)

YIELD: 120 COOKIES   **WRITTEN BY: CHRISTINE IT (CHRISTINE TSALAVOUTAS)**

2	cups vegetable oil
2	cups Crisco, melted
1	cup sugar
1	cup orange juice
4	eggs, (2 whole and 2 yolks)
1	shot cognac
	Orange rind (from 1 orange)
6	cups cake flour, sifted
2	tsp baking soda
2	tsp baking powder

1	TB cinnamon
1/4	tsp cloves
	Crushed walnuts for topping
1 1/2 cups honey	
1 1/2 cups sugar	
1 1/2 cups water	
	A lemon wedge
3	TB vanilla extract

Τα Μελομακάρονα της Θείας Μαρίας
Honey Dipped Cinnamon Cookies (Thea Maria's Melomakarona)

1. Place the first seven ingredients into a large mixer bowl. Mix until it thickens up and becomes a solid light brown color. In a small bowl, mix the baking soda, baking powder, cinnamon and cloves with two cups of the flour and blend this into the wet mixture. Mix thoroughly and start adding flour, a cup at a time, until batter is soft and full but not sticky.

2. Preheat oven to 350°F. Using an ice cream scoop drop cookies onto a parchment lined baking sheet. Place cookies, spacing them three across and six down, on two trays. I then use a fork to poke the top of the cookie two or three times on a slant, pressing the cookie down a bit. Use the top and middle racks and bake for 11 minutes then switch the trays and bake for 8 more minutes. Let the cookies cool before dipping them into the warm syrup.

3. Syrup: In a medium pot mix together the honey, sugar and water over medium heat. Add the lemon wedge and vanilla, and let it simmer. Once the syrup is clear and warm you can start dipping the cookies. Put the cookies in upside down letting them sit for about 30 seconds, flip them and let in for 30 seconds more. Remove with a slotted spoon and let cool. Sprinkle with crushed walnuts.

Christine Tsalavoutas is a proud mom and an amazing home cook. She started her own food blog, Christine It, so that family and friends could enjoy her recipes. Christine currently resides in Ontario, Canada. Check out www.christineitup.blogspot.com for more amazing recipes!

Ρυζόγαλο
Rice Pudding [Rizogalo]

SERVINGS: 4   **WRITTEN BY: MY EASY GOURMET (ELENI ANAGNOSTOPOULOU)**

4   TB arborio rice
1   glass water
4 1/4 cups milk
5   TB sugar
1   tsp vanilla extract
       Pinch of cinnamon
5   TB corn flour

1. Warm up the water in a large pot and add the rice, over medium heat.

2. Mix the corn flour with some cold milk in a mug and stir well until combined.

3. When the boiling water is absorbed by the rice, add the corn flour mix, the remaining milk, sugar and vanilla. Lower the heat to medium.

4. Stir occasionally as it gets thicker and remove from heat before it starts to boil.

5. Once the mixture has cooled down, pour into bowls and serve with a sprinkle of cinnamon. (You can enjoy warm or cold.)

Eleni, the food blogger at My Easy Gourmet, is not only an awesome photographer but an amazing food stylist too. She currently resides in Athens, Greece and rocking the kitchen with fusion Greek recipes. I met Eleni online, a few years back and my mind was blown away by her recipes. You can find her over at myeasygourmet.net

Fish & Seafood
Ψάρι & Θαλασσινά

Γαρίδες με Φέτα
Baked Shrimp & Feta

YIELD: 4

1	pinch Mediterranean seafood rub
1/4	lb. feta cheese
2	garlic cloves, minced
4	ounces olive oil
1	onion, finely chopped
1	tsp black pepper
1/2 tsp	pink Himalayan sea salt
1 3/4	lbs. shrimp
2	tomatoes, chopped

1. In a pan, sauté the onions in oil until translucent.

2. Add the tomatoes, garlic, and all the seasonings to the pan.

3. Simmer for 25 minutes. Prepare and clean the shrimp.

4. Place the shrimp in a baking dish and cover with the onion mixture. Sprinkle with feta on top.

5. Bake in oven at 375°F for 15 minutes, or until cheese has melted.

If you would like to add a slight sweetness to this dish, add a TB of honey.

In Greece this dish is typically served with toasted bread. Dip your bread in the tomato sauce and enjoy!

Γαύρος στο Φούρνο
Baked European Anchovies

YIELD: 5   WRITTEN BY: KICKING BACK THE PEBBLES (ATHINA PANTAZATOU)

2   pounds European anchovies
1   can of diced tomatoes
1   TB tomato paste
2   garlic cloves
2   cups fresh parsley, finely chopped
    Salt & pepper
    Dried oregano
    Pinch of sugar
2   TB olive oil
    Some finely chopped green garlic (young garlic) leaves to sprinkle with

1. Some people skip the cleaning part altogether and cook anchovies as are but my opinion is that, if you don't rinse & gut it, it will taste bitter! Use a small knife to squeeze gently into the underbelly and run it all the way up the gill area. Remove everything from the gut cavity and remove the gills and the head - which you may find coming off alongside the gills, on its own. Rinse any remains in the gut cavity under running water and let the fish drain for an hour or more (I use a colander over a large mixing bowl and place it in the fridge - I usually do it the night before).

2. Pour a little olive oil in an oven pan & lay your little fish in. Add salt, pepper and the dried oregano.

3. Finely chop the garlic and mix it into a bowl with the diced tomatoes, the tomato paste, the pinch of sugar and one cup of chopped parsley. Drizzle the sauce over your fish in the oven pan. Sprinkle over the remaining cup of fresh parsley.

4. Place rack in the center and make sure you preheat your oven. Then, bake at 390-430°F for 20-30 minutes. Sprinkle with fresh green garlic leaves and serve.

Γαρίδες στο Τηγάνι με Ντομάτα και Φέτα
Shrimp Saganaki

YIELD: 6   WRITTEN BY: FOODIE WINELOVER (GINA MARTINO ZARCADOOLAS)

2	lb. large shrimp, peeled and deveined, tails on
3	TB olive oil + more
8	garlic cloves, chopped
1	pint cherry tomatoes
2	tsp oregano
3/4	ounce ouzo
	Salt and black pepper to taste
6	oz. feta cheese, crumbled
	Flat leaf parsley, chopped for garnish

1. Place tomatoes on a tray, drizzle with olive oil and salt. Bake in a 375°F oven for 20-30 minutes, or until caramelized.

2. Meanwhile, in a "Saganaki" or large frying pan, heat olive oil over medium-high heat. Sauté the garlic for 1 minute and add the shrimp. Cook for about 3 minutes.

3. Deglaze with ouzo, turn the shrimp over, add the tomatoes, oregano, and black pepper.

4. Cook an additional 3 minutes, or until the shrimp are no longer translucent.

5. Garnish with parsley. Drizzle with olive oil. Serve with orzo, potatoes or pasta. I served mine with whole-wheat angel hair.

Be careful with the salt, as the feta is already salty.

If you don't have ouzo readily available, use some dry white wine, it will be the next best thing. However, in my opinion, ouzo is the way to go in this dish!

Gina Zarcadoolas shares memories of her Grandmother, Catherine Saba Jiha from Bethlehem-Palestine (Levant):

Catherine loved making Mahshi (stuffed cabbage), and Kibbeh (ground meat with cracked wheat). Her favorite cuisine was the Arabic.

Gina Martino Zarcadoolas is the name behind the blog Foodie WineLover. She's of Italian and Middle Eastern descent and grew up in the Caribbean. She's married to a Greek and loves to cook and entertain. Check out www.foodiewinelover.com for more amazing recipes!

Meat
Κρέας

BBQ Greek Chicken, pg 58

Κοτόπουλο Μπάρμπεκιου
BBQ Greek Chicken

YIELD: 7   WRITTEN BY: CHRISTINE IT (CHRISTINE TSALAVOUTAS)

7   chicken breasts

For the marinade, whisk together
1   cup of olive oil
1 1/2   lemons, juiced
1/2   tsp oregano
2   TB Greek seasoning
2   tsp salt
1   tsp pepper

1. Place the chicken breasts in a dish and pour the marinade on top. Make sure all the sides get coated and flip it every half hour.

2. Marinate the chicken for about 2 hours in the refrigerator.

3. While the chicken is marinating, make another half batch of the marinade to baste the chicken with while it is on the barbecue.

4. Place on barbecue, cook until chicken is done.

Κεφτέδες
Greek Meatballs [Keftedes]

YIELD: 20 KEFTEDES

4	slices of sour dough bread, crumbled
2	garlic cloves, minced
1	white onion, minced
1	bunch of fresh mint, chopped
1	bunch of fresh basil, minced
	Salt & pepper to taste
1/2	pound of ground beef
2	eggs
1/4	tsp of olive oil
1/2	cup of all-purpose flour
	Extra olive oil for the saucepan

1. In a food processor, add the onion, garlic, mint, basil, and seasonings. Mix. Add the onion mixture to a medium size bowl. Add in the bread crumbs and eggs. Mix again to combine and then add the olive oil.

2. Prepare a saucepan with olive oil over medium heat. Roll the mixture into 1 1/2 inch balls and place the balls into a plate with flour. Coat each meatball with flour and then dust it off slightly. Repeat the process until all the meat mixture is gone.

3. When the olive oil is hot, add about 4-5 meatballs at a time to the pan, and cook for about 10 minutes or until golden brown.

4. Drain on a paper towel when the meatballs are done. Serve with tzatziki & fresh lemon juice.

Μουσακάς
Eggplant Casserole [Moussaka]

YIELD: 15

2 cups olive oil	8 TB unsalted butter
5 bay leaves	1 cup flour
3 cinnamon sticks	4 cups milk
1 yellow onion, chopped	4 eggs, beaten
2 lb. ground beef	3 large eggplants cut into medium slices
1/2 cup tomato paste	1 cup Parmesan cheese
1 tsp ground cinnamon	
1 tsp ground nutmeg	
1 TB balsamic vinegar	
1 tsp honey	
1 tsp Himalayan salt	
1 can of chunky tomatoes	

1. Heat 3 tablespoons of olive oil in a large pan, over medium-high heat. Add bay leaves, cinnamon sticks, and onion. Cook for about 3 minutes or until the onion becomes translucent. Add the beef and brown it for about 25 minutes or so.

2. Add tomato paste, tomato chunks, 1/2 tsp. ground cinnamon, 1/2 tsp. ground nutmeg, balsamic vinegar, honey, and salt. Cook over medium heat, until liquid has reduced in half. Remove from heat and discard the bay leaves and cinnamon sticks.

3. **Béchamel Sauce:** Heat butter in a medium pot. Add flour; cook until smooth, about 2 minutes. Add 1 1/2 tsp. salt, remaining cinnamon and nutmeg, then milk; cook until thickened. Pour milk mixture into blender, add eggs. Blend until combined, set aside.

4. Prepare eggplants and sprinkle slices with cinnamon. Fry them in batches, in oil, until golden brown (about 10 minutes). Transfer to paper towels to have excess oil absorbed; set aside.

5. Spread 1/2 cup of béchamel in a large casserole dish. Sprinkle Parmesan cheese all over it and add half the beef mixture on top. Add eggplant slices and repeat all steps (béchamel-parmesan-beef-eggplant) until you have two or three layers. Make sure you finish with a béchamel layer on top. Bake for 1 hour at 350°F.

Σουτζουκάκια Σμυρνέικα
Greek Meatballs in Tomato Sauce [Soutzoukakia Smyrneika]

YIELD: 5   WRITTEN BY: CYTASTY (PANAYIOTIS GALANIS)

1 1/2	pounds minced beef
3	TB olive oil
4	garlic cloves
2	egg yolks
	Salt & pepper to taste
1	tsp cumin
	Chopped tomatoes
1	can tomato paste
2	TB ketchup

1. Put the mince in a bowl. Mash garlic cloves through a garlic press and add to minced meat. Separate the yokes of two eggs and add them to the minced meat along with the cumin, salt, and pepper. Knead until combined.

2. Put a tablespoon of olive oil in a frying pan. Roll the mince mixture into little sausage-like shapes with your hands and place them in the frying pan. Cook until brown.

3. Remove any fat with a spoon. Then add your chopped tomatoes, tomato paste, and tablespoon of ketchup.

4. Gently cook till the minced meat is cooked through but not so long as to let it get hard.

5. Serve over boiled rice with Greek "Horiatiki" salad.

Panayiotis Galanis, the wonderful food blogger over at CyTasty shares how it all started:

"I began my first Blog/Website in May 2014, when my daughter, Georgina, suggested I combined my enthusiasm for cooking, with my skills for writing articles, which I discovered I had, during my time in advertising sales, for local media. My first site was called 'Subject Spot' which was intended to be a broader spectrum of articles. But in December of 2014, I decided to hone in on my love for writing about my birthplace, Cyprus. Be it food recipes, its historic wines, produce or travel to there, I just can't write enough about the beautiful island of Cyprus, which is also reputed to be the birthplace of no less a deity than the goddess of love herself, Aphrodite. So came into existence 'CyTasty', which is my current website. The name can be interpreted in two ways, 'See Why It's Tasty' or 'Cyprus Tasty' with the play in the lettering of the name of the new Website." Check out Pany over at www.cytasty.com

Panagiotis Galanis shares memories of his Yiayia, Maria Cherkezou from Paralimni-Cyprus:

"I came to live in London with my parents in 1972, at the age of ten, having been born in Cyprus. I still remember a lot from those days, as a young child in Cyprus and some of my most vivid memories are from time spent with my yiayia and papou. My yiayia Maria's cooking was just so delicious and I remember pretty much every dish she used to make for us when we were visiting! 'Pizelia me kreas kokkinisto' (Peas with meat in tomato stew). The one dish I remember most is when yiayia was making her own halloumi and would serve us warm 'Anari' (soft cheese, a little like cottage cheese), which is a by-product of the halloumi making process. She would add a little sugar to it and sometimes a little cinnamon... simply delicious! My yiayia Maria was definitely a massive influence on my developing a self-taught culinary interest and part of why I developed my CyTasty food site."

Κοτόπουλο με Μακαρόνια
Stewed Chicken over Pasta

YIELD: 4

2	lbs. chicken breasts
1	cup olive oil
1	large onion, chopped
3	garlic cloves, chopped
2	cups tomatoes, chopped
1/4	cup red wine
1	cinnamon stick
2	bay leaves
1/4	tsp oregano
1/4	tsp basil
	Salt and pepper
2	cups chicken stock
1	lb. pasta, cooked
	Mizithra cheese

1. Rinse and dry the chicken pieces.

2. Place chicken breasts on a dry plate and add salt & pepper. In a large sauce pan, heat the oil.

3. Brown the chicken, onions, and garlic together.

4. Add the tomatoes, wine, chicken stock, bay leaves, and spices.

5. Let the chicken cook over low heat, until tender.

6. Prepare pasta, according to package directions. (I love to use fettuccine pasta, but you can use any kind of pasta you like).
Serve with fresh grated Mizithra, or Parmesan cheese.

Salads
Σαλάτες

Λαχανοσαλάτα
Cabbage & Carrot Salad [Lahanosalata]

YIELD: 2

- 1 green or red cabbage, cored and shredded
- 2 cups shredded carrots
- 3 TB olive oil
- 2 TB lemon juice
- 2 TB white vinegar
- 1 pinch oregano
  Salt & pepper

1. In a large mixing bowl, toss together the cabbage and carrots.

2. Whisk olive oil with lemon juice, apple cider vinegar and seasonings.

3. Pour over the cabbage mix and combine. Serve with fresh oregano sprinkled on top.

Σαλάτα Χωριάτικη
Greek Summer Salad [Horiatiki Salata]

YIELD: 2

4	ripe tomatoes
1	cucumber
1	onion
1	green pepper
1/3 lb.	strong feta cheese
	Kalamata olives
1/2 cup	olive oil
	Dried Greek oregano
1	lemon (juice)

1. Cut the vegetables in slices and mix in a salad bowl.

2. Top with the olives, oregano, lemon juice and cover with "crumbled" feta cheese.

3. Dress evenly with the olive.

If you have left over "salata", you can make a simple appetizer called Dakos. Dakos is a Cretan specialty. Simply take slices of any kind of bread, such as sourdough, and toast them in the oven, brushed with olive oil. Add a tablespoon of the salad mixture over the top and enjoy!

Side Note: We call this a "horiatiki" salad (horiatiki means "of a village")because it was a very common, summer-time salad, often consumed in the rural parts of Greece, the villages, where farmers always had the simplest yet freshest ingredients on hand. Fresh tomatoes straight from the patch, cucumbers, onions, peppers, oregano, lemon juice and olive oil (no lettuce). It is not a true Greek Summer Salad if it has lettuce in it!

Σαλάτα με Καρπούζι & Φέτα
Watermelon Feta Salad

YIELD: 2   WRITTEN BY: MY EASY GOURMET (ELENI ANAGNOSTOPOULOU)

4	cups watermelon
3/4	cup feta cheese
1	small red onion
1/4	cup mint leaves
1/4	cup parsley
4	TB olive oil
1	TB lime juice
	Black sesame seeds

1. Remove the seeds from the watermelon.

2. Cut the watermelon and feta in cubes. Chop the mint leaves, parsley, and onion.

3. Assemble the salad. Season with olive oil and lime juice.

4. Garnish with sesame seeds.

Soups
Σούπες

Σούπα Αυγολέμονο
Chicken Lemon Soup [Avgolemono]

YIELD: 4

1	whole chicken	1/2	cup rice
12	cups water	3	eggs
2	carrots, diced	2	tsp fresh lemon zest
2	celery stalks, diced		Juice of two lemons, strained
1	large onion, diced		Salt and pepper
2	bay leaves	1	pinch cumin
5	whole black peppercorns	1	pinch oregano
2	tsp salt	1	pinch dill

1. Add the first eight ingredients to a big pot. Bring the water to a boil and then lower heat to medium/low. Cover and let boil for about an hour or an hour and a half.

2. Remove the chicken and vegetables into a bowl and strain the broth out. Return the broth to the pot and bring to a boil again. Add the rice to the pot and keep on boiling (keep the pot uncovered this time!) for about 10 minutes, until the rice is soft. While the rice is cooking, start preparing the sauce.

3. Using a whisk beat the eggs until frothy. Add the lemon zest and lemon juice. I like to go crazy with lemon so I tend to add a bit more. Continue to whisk.

4. When the rice is ready, turn off the heat. Ladle about 2 cups of the broth into a small bowl. This is the tricky part so make sure you do this slowly! Add the hot broth into your lemon-egg mixture while whisking continuously. I like to do this pretty fast so

the egg doesn't curdle into the broth but if it is your first time then, please, just do this slowly so as to be extra careful and make sure you don't burn yourself!

5. Stir the egg-lemon-broth mixture back into the pot. Simmer over very low heat for approximately 5 minutes. Remove from heat and add salt and pepper to taste. To serve, sprinkle some freshly chopped dill on top.

Τραχανάς Σούπα
Trahanas Soup

YIELD: 4   WRITTEN BY: MY EASY GOURMET (ELENI ANAGNOSTOPOULOU)

1	cup trahanas (you can find trahanas at any Greek market)
1/2	cup tomato juice
4	cups vegetable stock
2	TB butter
	Salt and pepper
	Feta cheese and bread for serving

1. Melt the butter in a large pot under medium heat.

2. Add all the ingredients, season with salt and pepper and cook for 10 minutes.

3. Stir occasionally, and serve with crumbled feta cheese.

Γιουβαρλάκια από Κιμά Γαλοπούλας
Youvarlakia with Turkey Meat

YIELD: 4

3	cups chicken broth		2	TB fresh parsley, finely chopped
1/2	cup all-purpose flour		2	garlic cloves, chopped
1	pinch fresh oregano		1	white onion, finely chopped
1	pinch cumin		1/3	cup rice (uncooked)
1	large egg		1	lb. ground turkey/ beef
	Ground pepper			
	Sea salt		4	lemons (juice)
1	TB fresh anise, finely chopped		3	large eggs
2	TB fresh dill, finely chopped			

1. In a large bowl, combine: Meat, rice, onion, garlic, cumin, dill, anise, parsley, salt, pepper and egg.

2. Place flour on a plate, form meatballs in your hand and gently roll into the flour.

3. Place the meatballs in a large pot and pour the chicken broth over them.

4. Bring to a boil. Cover and simmer for about 40 minutes. In the meantime prepare the avgolemono.

5. In a large bowl add the eggs and whisk until nice and frothy. Add the lemon juice, and season with salt and pepper.

6. The meatballs should be ready by now, so prepare to combine the avgolemono with the meatballs.

7. Take two half cups of hot broth and quickly whisk the broth into the avgolemono sauce. Be sure to do this quickly as the eggs can curdle if you don't. Add the avgolemono mixture to the meatballs and mix to combine.

Spices & Teas
Τσάι & Μπαχαρικά

Ελαιόλαδο Αρωματισμένο με Άνηθο
Dill Oil

1/4   cup extra virgin olive oil
1/2   cup dill leaves

Perfect on chicken, fish, and pasta salads.

1. Place the olive oil in a skillet over medium heat.

2. Heat oil until it is warm.

3. Add dill to the skillet and let it sit for 20 minutes.

4. Place the olive oil and dill in a blender, and process until smooth.

Μείγμα Ελληνικών Μπαχαρικών
Greek Seasoning Mix

2	tsp dried oregano
2	tsp sea salt
1 1/2	tsp onion powder
1 1/2	tsp garlic powder
2	tsp dried basil
1	tsp paprika
1/2	tsp cinnamon
1/2	tsp thyme
1	pinch black pepper

Combine all ingredients and store in an air-tight container.

Perfect on fish, chicken, vegetables and more!

Τσάι του Βουνού
Mountain Tea [Chai Tou Vounou]

1/3 cup chamomile, flowers and stems
1 pot water
Honey
Lemon

1. Boil the flowers, stems and water for 5 minutes.

2. Strain out the flowers and stems, add honey and lemon.

This unique tea is originally made of dried flowers and stems from the plant Sideritis Syriaca (Ironwort). Sideritis means "of" or "with iron". This type of tea is believed to be the reason why the people of the Greek villages, who largely consumed it, lived up to a 100 years old!

Τσάι Βανίλια
Vanilla Chai

SERVES: 2

1 1/2	cups water
1 1/3	cup milk
1	TB black tea
1	cinnamon stick
1	tsp clove
1/4	tsp all spice
1/4	tsp cardamom
1	vanilla bean, cut in half
1	tsp dried ginger
1	orange peel
3	TB honey

1. Place water and spices into a large pot (except from the tea).

2. Cook over medium heat, for about 5 minutes.

3. Add black tea and steep for another 5 minutes.

4. Slowly add in the milk and remove from stove.

5. Strain out the spices and add honey.

Herbs and teas date back to the ancient times in Greece. Greece is famous for its unique herbs and spices, so it is not surprising that Greek cuisine encompasses many different flavors from an assortment of herbs.

Herbs flourish on the islands of Greece. Listed below are some of the most popular spices found in Greece.

Anise: Glykaniso/Glykanisos
Basil: Vasilikos
Cinnamon: Kanela
Celeriac: Selino
Chamomile: Hamomili
Coriander: Coliandro
Dill: Anithos
Fennel: Maratho/Marathos
Lavender: Levanda

Marjoram: Madzourana
Mint: Diosmos
Oregano: Rigani
Parsley: Maédanos
Rosemary: Dendrolivano
Sage: Faskomilo
Thyme: Thymari

Vegetables
Λαχανικά

Αγγινάρες αλα Πολίτα
Artichokes with Lemon Sauce [Aginares ala Polita]

YIELD: 5

6	large artichokes
4	lemons
2	garlic cloves, minced
1	white onion, chopped
2	cups carrots, diced
4	large potatoes, peeled and cubed
2	TB flour
1	cup olive oil
1/4	cup water
	Salt and pepper
	Fresh dill to sprinkle with

1. Prepare artichokes by removing outer layers of leaves. Remove hearts and set aside. (Discard leaves and outer layers).

2. Add 1/4 cup olive oil in a large pan, over medium heat. Sauté onions, carrots and garlic for a few minutes until the onions are translucent.

3. Add the potatoes and continue to sauté.

4. Whisk olive oil with lemon juice, flour and water. Add to the pan.

5. Bring to a boil, then reduce heat and simmer for about 25 minutes.

6. Add the artichokes and season with salt and pepper.

7. Cook for an additional 15 minutes or so.

8. Garnish with fresh dill over the top. Serve over rice.

Μπριάμ
Greek Baked Vegetables [Briam]

YIELD: 5   WRITTEN BY: CHRISTINE IT (CHRISTINE TSALAVOUTAS)

1	medium eggplant
	Salt and pepper
2	medium red onions
4	large garlic cloves
3 1/2	large potatoes, peeled
2	zucchinis
3	large bell peppers
1	cup green beans
2/3	cup olive oil (Extra Virgin)
1	can tomato sauce
1/4	cup chopped parsley (optional)
2	TB chopped marjoram (optional)
1	cup feta, crumbled

1. Cut everything up and layer vegetables in a deep roasting pan. Pour the tomato sauce over the vegetables and generously drizzle olive oil on top. Sprinkle with fresh spices. Mix everything together.

2. Cook uncovered in the oven at 400°F and, after approximately 45 minutes, stir the vegetables carefully to bring all the bottom ones up to the top. Cook until desired tenderness is reached. Once the briam has cooled, sprinkle with fresh feta.

Σκορδαλιά
Greek Mashed Potatoes [Skordalia]

YIELD: 5

8	garlic cloves
1	pound of potatoes
1	cup olive oil
3	TB red wine vinegar
3	TB lemon juice
	Cyprus flake salt

1. Prepare the potatoes, peel and cut into cubes. Place potatoes in salted boiling water. Once boiled, drain water and let cool.

2. In a food processor, process the garlic cloves, olive oil, and salt.

3. Hand mix the potatoes, making sure they are well combined. Add the garlic-olive oil paste to the potatoes and whisk together. Add the lemon juice and red wine vinegar to the potatoes. Chill skordalia for a few hours so the flavors can combine.

4. When ready to serve, sprinkle some fresh dill on top.

Skordalia is perfect with fish and chicken

Σπανακόρυζο
Spinach & Rice [Spanakorizo]

YIELD: 6

1	pound of fresh spinach
1	cup Swiss chard
1/4	cup olive oil
1	cup fresh onion, finely chopped
1	leek, finely chopped
2	garlic cloves, finely chopped
1	lemon (juice and zest)
1/4	cup fresh dill, chopped
1/4	cup fresh basil, chopped
1/4	cup fresh mint, chopped
2	tsp oregano
1	cup Basmati rice (uncooked)
3	cups water
1 1/2	tsp sea salt
1	pinch ground cumin
1	pinch black pepper
	Balsamic vinegar

1. Heat olive oil in large pan over medium heat.

2. Sauté onions and leeks until they become translucent (about 5 minutes).

3. Add garlic and sauté for 1 minute.

4. Add lemon zest, dill, basil, mint, oregano, cumin, Swiss chard, and spinach. Cook until the spinach has wilted down.

5. Stir in the rice and water. Bring to a boil.

6. Reduce the heat and place the lid over the pan. Let the rice cook for approximately 20 minutes.

7. When the mixture has cooled, stir in the lemon juice and balsamic vinegar.

8. Enjoy with some fresh feta on top.

Do what you love and follow your heart.

Don't be afraid to follow your passions and work hard towards your goals. If you fail the first time, don't worry. You must start from the bottom and work your way up!

Don't ever let anyone take your dreams away from you. Remember to listen to your heart.

It was not easy for me to start Kouzounas Kitchen, but I knew that I wanted to share the love of Greek food with my family and friends. So the next best thing was to start a blog. I have been happily blogging for almost 3 years now, and I have met with some wonderful people from all around the world.

The best part about my job as a chef is I get to put a smile on people's faces. I have been fortunate to cater for weddings, corporate events, bridal and baby showers and much, much more. My friends ask me, "How do you do it, super woman??" I laugh and say, "This is my true passion; to cook, it's in my Greek blood."

I will end this book with one of my favorite quotes:

"A recipe has no soul, you as the cook,
must bring soul to the recipe."
– Julia Child (1912-2004)

INDEX